FEASTS OF JEHOVAH

FEASTS *of* JEHOVAH

JOHN RITCHIE

JOHN RITCHIE LTD
CHRISTIAN PUBLICATIONS

40 Beansburn, Kilmarnock, Scotland

ISBN 0 946351 92 9

Copyright © 2000 by John Ritchie Ltd.
40 Beansburn, Kilmarnock, Scotland

Typeset by John Ritchie Ltd., Kilmarnock
Printed by Bell & Bain Ltd., Glasgow

Contents

Publishers' Preface

Feasts of Jehovah is one of the books written by Mr John Ritchie about one hundred years ago, by means of which several generations of believers have been introduced to the rich pastures of Old Testament typical teaching. In the belief that such teaching is timeless in its relevance and applicability, John Ritchie Ltd has commissioned and produced this new edition in a style, format and language suited to present day readers. They are grateful to Dr Bert Cargill for his work in editing and revising this book to make it available in this form.

What was the purpose and origin of these Feasts of Jehovah described here? Were they just ceremonial occasions throughout the old Jewish calendar, breaking up the year and providing opportunity for family gatherings and national celebrations? Did they only commemorate some important events in the nation's history, as the Passover certainly did? Or was there a much deeper and more lasting reason for these feasts being instituted and continued down the centuries? Is there benefit for us in studying them? Do they have a spiritual meaning and application to us?

Answers to these questions, and other details of great interest, are to be found in the following pages. Readers will find rich spiritual refreshment, as their minds and hearts are directed to the Lord Jesus to whom every ceremony and type in the Old Testament unmistakably point. The past, the present, and the future, redemption, grace and glory, are all covered in the study of these seven feasts of Jehovah. Great benefit will also be obtained by reading along with this one, John Ritchie's companion volumes entitled *Egypt to Canaan* and *The Tabernacle in the Wilderness*.

The short chapters of this book are self-contained studies of topics of spiritual value, as we move through the calendar of the nation of Israel, noting the origin of each of the seven Feasts of Jehovah, their spiritual lessons and what will be their prophetic fulfilment. God's great plans and His eternal purpose are here foreshadowed, all centred on the person and work of His beloved Son, Christ Jesus our Lord. By His grace, we have been included in these, therefore our minds should be stirred to understand, and hearts and to worship, as we have brought to our attention the details of these ancient Feasts and their spiritual and eternal significance.

John Ritchie Ltd
Kilmarnock

CHAPTER 1

Introduction

As we read through the four Gospels with which the New Testament commences, we frequently find that certain events in the life of our Lord Jesus Christ took place at Jewish Feasts or Festivals. There was, for example, the Passover referred to in Luke 2:41 to which He travelled with His parents when He was twelve years old. Another memorable Passover is referred to in John 12:1 and 13:1, and in the later chapters of each of the other Gospels. Before it He met with those who loved Him, first at supper in the house at Bethany and then in the upper room in Jerusalem. But on its very date He was taken by those who hated Him and He was led out to die at Calvary as the Lamb of God, bearing away the sin of the world, for that was God's appointed time. The commentary on this unique event given by the apostle Paul later is that "Christ our passover is sacrificed for us" (1 Cor 5:7).

Another feast, the Feast of Tabernacles, is referred to in John 7:2. It was the last one of the year, and on its eighth and last and greatest day, Jesus stood and cried, "If any man thirst, let him come unto Me and drink" (v.37). That which ceremonial observances could not supply to the seeking, thirsty soul He could and would, to all who came to Him, and indeed to all who still come to Him. They would then become channels of His blessing to others, in the power of the Holy Spirit who would be given when Jesus was glorified (v.39).

These two examples indicate to us that such "Feasts of Jehovah" have a deeper significance. We shall return to this later in this book and explore it in detail. But first we must go back to the Old Testament to find the origin of the feasts and the circumstances in which they were instituted.

The main chapter which gives details of them all is Leviticus 23. It gives an account of seven great feasts which Jehovah commanded His people Israel to observe annually in the land of Canaan. As we shall see, this chapter of God's Word contains in type and in figure, a record of God's dealings with man in grace, from the death of Christ right on to His millennial kingdom, and to the eternal glory and rest which lie beyond it. It is also a prophecy, and a foreshadowing of some great events of the future, some of which have since been fulfilled, and some of which are yet to be.

The "Feasts of Jehovah" all pointed onward to subjects of eternal interest; subjects on which the mind and heart of God - Father, Son, and Holy Spirit - had been engaged before the world was made. In due time and order, they would take their places in that marvellous chain of events, which when completed will show the infinite wisdom and love of God, in all His purposes of grace towards the sons of men.

They are each a "shadow of things to come", of which Christ is the "body" (Col 2:17) or substance ; foreshadowings of His peerless person, and infinitely precious work, over which all true believers delight to meditate, on which by faith they feed, and which they find to be the strength and joy of their spiritual life. As we meditate on this great chapter in the Word of God, our souls will be fed, our spiritual strength and vigour increased, and our hearts drawn towards God, towards Christ His blessed Son, and towards heaven, our glorious home for ever.

Many of the subjects which we will consider here will be

familiar to those who have known the Lord and enjoyed His Word for many years. For the truths of this chapter in Leviticus are all cardinal truths of our most holy faith, the very foundations of Christianity, the solid rocks on which the faith and hope of saints all through the ages have rested. Although they are old they are also ever new, and their re-stating is always welcome to those who have known them longest and best. But it may be there are young ones in the flock of Christ, "little children" (1 John 2:12) of the family of God, to whom these great and precious themes will be less familiar. A patient study of these will be a means of establishing and strengthening young believers, in a day of uncertainty and conflicting teaching, a day in which the enemy of our souls is seeking to carry the battle to the very centre of the camp, and assail if he can, the foundations of our faith.

As we begin to read Leviticus 23, one of the first things we must notice is that these feasts are "Feasts of Jehovah", or "Jehovah's Feasts". The word used for *feasts* in v.2 means "to meet by appointment", so that some have translated it "set feasts" (RV) or "appointed seasons" (Newberry). So Jehovah was the host, His people were the guests. He ordained these feasts as celebrations of His own joy and His own delight in the great events to which they pointed, and of which they were the foreshadowing types. Yes, they were *His* feasts, and by them we may understand what it is that *He* delights in and where *His* enjoyments are to be found - things which He now wants to share with us!

The various feasts which we will consider from the Scriptures, now interpreted and understood in the light of their antitypes, reveal to us what has afforded joy and delight for ages past to the God of heaven, and what will still supply the joy of heaven in ages yet to come. How poor and miserable are the subjects that occasion mirth and gladness among men on earth compared with these! And how soon those fade away, and are forgotten! But heaven's enjoyments last; they do not lose their charm. The person and the work of Christ retain their fragrance, and will for ever continue to give to all heaven an object to gaze upon, and a subject to sing of. After earth's songs have all been sung, its joys all ended, its mirth all passed away, heaven's "Hallelujah Psalm" will continue to be sung by radiant hosts in immortal youth around the throne of God.

Jehovah's set Feasts were also "holy convocations" (v.2), that is a "calling together" of His people. He did not keep all His joys to Himself - He shared them with His redeemed people. He called them together around Himself to be joint-partakers with Him of His joy. How wonderful this is! But how much more wonderful is God's present grace to His heavenly people. Our God is not a lonely being, like the God of the Unitarian or of the Mohammedan, He is a God of fellowship. He delights to have His people sharing His joys, and finding their delights in Christ, in whom His own delights are all found. This is fellowship. This is what the saints have been called to: to share God's thoughts of Christ; to find their rest with Him in Christ. This is our calling - it ought to be our experience and enjoyment. Does the world deprive us of it ? Do earthly things so occupy and engross our thoughts and affections, that the things of God and of Christ get little attention? Do business and worldly cares so monopolise our days and hours that there is no energy, no time left, to think of and delight in God and His Christ? May we have more *heart* for this, and make time available so that we may enjoy it, indeed enjoy *Him*, as our God wants us to.

CHAPTER 2

The Redeemed of the Lord

"Happy art thou, O Israel; who is like unto thee, O people saved by the Lord" (Deut 33:29).

"The children of Israel, a people near unto Him" (Psa 148:14).

> *No longer far from Him, but now*
> *By 'precious blood' made nigh;*
> *'Accepted' in the well-Beloved,*
> *Near to God's heart we lie.*

Before looking at the feasts in the order in which they are recorded, it will be helpful to pause for a moment and reflect upon the history of the people to whom these instructions were given. We also need to consider where, and at what period of their history, these commandments from Jehovah reached them.

The preceding book, the book of Exodus, opens with a picture of this people, the Israelites, in Egypt as slaves in bondage, serving Pharaoh and his gods. No "Feasts of Jehovah", no holy convocations or times of rejoicing were known by them there. They were slaves and idolaters. This shows us man in his natural state: unregenerate, unconverted man, away from God, in the world and belonging to it, serving Satan, its "god" and "prince". But to this miserable and downtrodden people, redemption and deliverance came. They were brought out of Egypt, separated from its people and its idolatries, to become the chosen people of Jehovah.

Listen to God's word to them: "Ye have seen what I did unto the Egyptians, and how I bare you on eagle's wings, and brought you unto Myself" (Exod 19:4). They were delivered from the rule and authority of Pharaoh, to be Jehovah's "peculiar treasure", a people "near unto Him" (Psa 148:14), a people "not reckoned among the nations", but dwelling alone (Num 23:9), with Jehovah in their midst, shielding, protecting, and ruling over them. No wonder that Moses, the man of God, in taking his farewell of them as they encamped on the last stage of their wilderness journey, uttered the memorable words: "Happy art thou, O Israel: who is like unto thee, O people saved by the Lord" (Deut 33:29). The position, and the blessings of Israel as the redeemed of Jehovah, are but shadows of the still higher and wealthier place into which all believers of this age are brought "in Christ", as described in the glowing words of the apostle, "Blessed be the God and Father of our Lord Jesus Christ, who bath blessed us with *all spiritual blessings* in heavenly *places* in Christ" (Eph 1:3).

Now less than this might have satisfied us - to be delivered from hell and judgment was all that *we* desired in our unconverted days. But less could not satisfy our God, or fulfil the desires of His heart. His purpose was to have a people near unto Him, a family around Himself, beautiful in His eyes, all "holy and without blame before Him in love" (Eph 1:4).

So as we proceed into the book of Leviticus, we see that Jehovah gave Israel these commandments concerning His feasts after they had been brought completely out from Egypt and gathered around Him in the wilderness, with His presence in their midst and His cloud hovering over them. He was then able to reveal to them what was in His heart, and to invite them to share with Him the great things which had been the subjects of His thoughts from eternal ages. Leviticus 23 would have been of no use to them in Egypt. Other interests occupied them while they were there, but now they are alone in the desert, separated unto God as the subjects of His redeeming grace and power. Now He is able to tell out His heart's desire. And they, no longer occupied with Egypt's sins and follies, no longer groaning for deliverance, but standing in the full enjoyment of Jehovah's salvation, are able to hear and respond to these desires of His heart.

So it is with the people of God today. Individually, we are called to have fellowship with the Father and the Son (1 John 1:3); and collectively, the church - the "called out" and "called together" company of God's saints, is called unto the fellowship of God's Son, "Jesus Christ our Lord" (1 Cor 1:9). All of this most clearly shows how delightful it is to God to share with His people now all that gives joy and gladness to His own heart. What a marvel of divine grace and love!

Now just in passing, and in contrast to all this, let us look at what we find in John 2:13; 5:1; 7:2. During the life of the Lord Jesus on earth, these feasts were still being observed by the Jewish people in the city of Jerusalem, the place where God's temple stood. Crowds from all parts of the country came up to Jerusalem to keep the Passover, the Feast of Pentecost, and the Feast of Tabernacles. But notice what the Lord Jesus calls them: no longer His feasts, but "feasts of the Jews". The outward form was there, but Jehovah's joy in them had ceased. Speaking of them earlier in their history, He had said, "*Your* new moons and *your* appointed feasts My soul hateth: they are a trouble to Me; I am weary to bear them" (Isa 1:14). And this was because of the formal manner in which a defiled and corrupted people observed them.

Surely, beloved children of God, we may learn from this a searching and solemn lesson: when the heart is away from God, hands defiled by sin, feet ceasing to walk in the truth, then an empty form of worship is only a farce and a sham. How much religion there is in our day, perhaps of great account in the eyes of men, highly esteemed and loudly praised, which a holy God finds a weariness. His soul hates it, and with it He will not connect His Name. Let us keep a jealous watch on our hearts - the source of all departure from God is there - lest of us He may have to say, "My soul shall have no pleasure in him" (Heb 10:38).

At the beginning, Jehovah was so desirous that His people should approach Him three times each year at these "set feasts", happy and without care, that He pledged His word to look after their earthly interests while they did so. He would care for their wives, their children, and their land, all the time they were at Jerusalem keeping His feasts. We all know how very difficult it is to rejoice before the Lord, and to worship Him joyfully, when household cares and business worries are pressing like a burden on the mind. No doubt Jehovah knew that when the men of Israel went up to keep the feasts, leaving all behind them, the thought might often disturb them, "What if the Philistines invade the country while we are away, and take possession of our fields? What if our houses are spoiled and our possessions are stolen?" And so He gave them a special promise that during their absence no one would be allowed to take away or even desire their possessions: "Neither shall any man desire thy land when thou shalt go to appear before the Lord thy God thrice in the year" (Exod 34:24). Blessed be His Name! – He took care of everything.

In a similar way the same God says to us now, "Gather My saints together unto Me", and He forbids His people to forsake "the assembling of ourselves together" (Heb 10:25). And He will surely make it His care to see that those who heartily obey His command shall not be losers for time or eternity by so doing. Yet, alas! on our part how often a passing shower of rain, a slight illness, or a domestic duty, is sufficient excuse for our absence from the Lord's Supper and for neglect of the worship of God. But the promises of God remain the same, and all who give the Lord what is His due will find them fulfilled: "Them that honour Me, I will honour" (1 Sam 2:30); "Seek ye first the kingdom of God, and His righteousness (that is, give God what He asks for, make His demands your first concern) and all these things shall be added unto you" (Matt 6:33).

A final lesson comes to us from Leviticus 23. As Jehovah was the host, and His people the guests, all the arrangements regarding the time, the place, and the ordering of the feasts, were undertaken by Himself alone. Nothing was left to the people to arrange by their own ideas or by vote or anything else. Divine legislation provided for the whole. Happy had it been for those people of God of long ago if they had been content with the divine commandments concerning their convocations, and that they added nothing to them in their traditions, but alas they did. And happy surely will it be with Christians now, if in their church order and their worship, they cleave to and follow the Word of God. Had this been done, human creeds and "confessions of faith", with their resulting divisions and barriers, would have been unknown and unnecessary. All God's saints would be found of one heart and one soul, as they were in Acts 4:32, guided by one Book, governed by one Head, themselves happy and peaceful, and a powerful united testimony for God in the midst of an evil world.

CHAPTER 3

The Seven Feasts

"These are the set feasts of Jehovah " (Lev 23:4, RV).
"A shadow of things to come" (Col 2:17).

> *Blessed table, where the Lord*
> *Sets for us His choicest cheer:*
> *Angels hath no feast like this,*
> *Angels serve, but cannot share.*

Before going on to consider the different feasts, and to gather the great doctrinal and practical lessons God has designed them to teach us, you should look at the diagram at the end of this book, on which these feasts are tabulated in the order in which they occurred.

The feasts are seven in number, or, if we include the Sabbath, there are eight. The Sabbath must be considered separately from the rest, for it is different in its character and in the frequency of its observance. It was observed weekly whilst the rest of the feasts were observed annually. It could be kept at home, whilst all the others must be observed at "the place which the Lord had chosen in which to place His name" (Deut 12:14; 16:5-6).

You will notice that Leviticus 23 opens with the words, "concerning the feasts of Jehovah" (v.2). Then after giving commandment about the Sabbath in v.3, the statement, "These are the set feasts of Jehovah" occurs again, making as it were, a fresh beginning. Then the seven feasts are described without a further repetition of these words throughout the chapter. Thus, while the Sabbath stands alone, the other seven follow in sequence and have a certain relation to each other. Although the Sabbath is first mentioned, it is last in being fulfilled. The other feasts have or will have their fulfilment as time rolls its course, whilst all that the Sabbath speaks of, can only be known in its fullness throughout eternity.

The seven Feasts may be divided into two groups, four in one group and three in the other. The first group is made up of the Passover, the Feast of Unleavened Bread, the Feast of First-fruits, and the Feast of Pentecost, each following the other closely in the early part of the year. Then there was an interval of four months, during which there was no "feast of Jehovah" and no "holy convocation" of the people at Jerusalem. A long interval or pause occurred between the Feast of Pentecost and the next feast, during which no fresh call from Jehovah to His people was heard. After that the Feast of Trumpets, the Feast of the Day of Atonement, and the Feast of Tabernacles followed each other in the seventh month of the year, making up the second group of three feasts.

This is significant and instructive. The meaning of it seems to be that the truths foreshadowed in the first four feasts are all connected with the *present* age, and with the calling out from the world those who are the *heavenly* people of the Lord, and form the body of Christ. The last three feasts foreshadow *future* mercies and times of blessing which are in store for Jehovah's *earthly* people, the nation of Israel, as well as for His heavenly people of this present time. In other words, the first four speak of and to the church, the body of Christ, while the latter three speak of Jehovah's future dealings with His earthly people, the seed of Abraham, the nation of His choice, who will be gathered again to their own land in the latter days, in covenant relation with God for earthly blessing under Messiah their king.

God ordained these feasts as celebrations of His own joy in the great events to which they pointed, and invited His redeemed and chosen people to gather together and share His joys with Him. He has fulfilled these types completely and to the very letter in what has already come to pass. This surely warrants the expectation that He will as surely in His own due time fulfil what yet remains. For the purposes of God stand fast, and can never be disannulled by the perversities and failures of men. A chapter like Leviticus 23 should confirm and strengthen our faith in the sacred and infallible Word of God. It is so full of the glorious gospel of God, so replete with types and teachings on the foundations of the faith. It is all so clearly the inspiration of the eternal God, speaking of things beforehand which He has purposed should come to pass. The great battle waged by infidelity and so-called science continues against the Book of God, seeking to undo faith's grip and raise doubts and questions as to its credibility. But the words of the Lord are pure words. They will stand up to being examined with microscopic care. And the more they are thus examined in the fear of God, the stronger will the evidences appear on every page that they are what they claim to be, the God-breathed words (*theopneusta,* 2 Tim 3:16) of Him who cannot lie.

Three times in the year all the males of Israel were commanded to appear before the Lord their God: at the Passover, the Feast of Weeks or Pentecost, and the Feast of Tabernacles (see Exodus 23:14-17), in the place where the Lord had placed His Name (Deut 16:16). With what joy and gladness the thousands of Israel out of all their tribes, from all parts of the goodly land, assembled there to rejoice before Jehovah, and to give back to Him His portion out of the fullness of the blessing which He had given them (Deut 16:17).

The little cluster of Psalms 122-134, called "Songs of Degrees", are believed to have been chanted by the crowds of joyful pilgrims, as they journeyed up to the "city of the great King", Jerusalem, which was "beautiful for situation, the joy of the whole earth", in the palaces of which God was known "for a refuge" (Psa 48:2-3). While the people of the Lord were right in heart, they rejoiced to the full in these gatherings, and were glad as they said one to another, "Let us go into the house of the Lord" (Psa 122:1). But when they got away in heart from their God, they found His commandments grievous, and soon neglected them. How dim the fine gold had become in the days of Malachi's prophecy when none would open a door or kindle a fire in God's house for nought (1:10), when the blind and the lame were offered in sacrifice (1:8), and when Jehovah's worship and service had become "a weariness" (1:13).

The answer to this in our day is easily found. When saints are right in heart with their God, in the freshness of spiritual affection, nothing is deemed too costly or too great for Him. Our heart's song then is

> "Nought that I have mine own I call,
> I hold it for the Giver;
> My heart, my strength, my life, my all,
> Are His, and His for ever."

Our feet are swift in running His errands, our hands are diligent doing His work; joy and gladness shine in our very countenance. This condition may mark us through life to the journey's end, and the Lord wants it to be. There is no necessity and no provisions made for decline or deterioration in our attitude to the things of God. The saint may be fresh and green even in old age, like the palm-tree, ever yielding fruit.

When we come to New Testament times, we do not find the many feasts of former times continued into the present age of grace. There is now only one feast given to the church, one holy convocation of saints. That feast is the Lord's Supper. That gathering in which it takes place is the *"ecclesia"*, the assembled church. Just as the seven feasts of Jehovah pointed onward to Christ, and were foreshadowings of redemption and glory to come, so the Lord's Supper looks backward to the cross of Christ and onward to His glory. It is the memorial of Christ's death, and the pledge of His coming again. We find that it actually embraces within itself all that was typified in these seven feasts of Jehovah as follows.

- The bread and wine are the memorials of Christ's death. This is the answer to *the Passover.*

- The communion of saints in holiness and love, gathered around the table feeding together on Christ, is the answer to the *Feast of Unleavened Bread.*

- The presence of the risen Lord Jesus in the midst of His own while they remember Him, is the answer to *the Feast of Firstfruits.* They are even now risen with Him (Col 3:1), having died and been buried with Him in baptism (2:12).

- The one Body of Christ formed and indwelt by the Spirit of God; the gathered saints "builded together for an habitation of God in the Spirit" (Eph 2:22); the Holy Spirit present to guide in worship and ministry, to take of the things of Christ and present them to the gathered worshippers, answers to *Pentecost.*

- The feast continued "till He come" (1 Cor 11:26) directs the eye of hope to a great and glorious future, the coming of the Lord to awaken the sleeping saints, to change the living, and to gather all together around Himself. The Judgement Seat to review and reward all faithful service for the Lord, the bright beams of millennial glory, and the glorious reign of Christ and His people over a peaceful world, all are anticipated by a heavenly people in the fulfilment of the *Feast of Trumpets,* the *Atonement* and the joyful *Feast of Tabernacles.* Their meaning and their message to the "blinded" earthly people are meantime unheard and unheeded.

Thus on the first day of the week, the saints assemble around their Lord, gather in His peerless name to break the bread and drink the wine for a remembrance of Him. They meditate upon Him, and in spirit view all these wondrous scenes which are the strength and joy of the new man. May we ever have hearts to value and enjoy these privileges worthily. As one who knew them well sang long ago, and has left for our hearts and lips, may we also truly sing,

> *"To Calvary, Lord, in spirit now*
> *Our joyful souls repair,*
> *To dwell upon Thy dying love,*
> *And taste its sweetness there.*
>
> *Sweet resting place of every heart*
> *That feels the plague of sin;*
> *Yet knows that deep, mysterious joy,*
> *The peace of God within.*
>
> *Thy sympathies and hopes are ours,*
> *We long, O Lord to see*
> *Creation all below, above,*
> *Redeemed and blessed by Thee."*

CHAPTER 4

The Sabbath

"The seventh day is the Sabbath of rest" (Lev 23:3).

"There remaineth therefore a Sabbath-rest for the people of God" (Heb 4:9 RV).

> *That rest secure from ill,*
> *No cloud of grief ere stains,*
> *Unfailing praise each heart doth fill,*
> *And love eternal reigns.*

The Sabbath, standing as it does at the beginning of this great typical chapter, has a place and a character of its own. It was observed weekly all through the year, even while the other feasts were in progress and also when they were not. It had an existence long before any of them, even as far back as Genesis 2, and all the time it had been bringing its weekly day of rest to the weary sons of Adam's toiling race.

The Sabbath was "a shadow of things to come" (Col 2:17), a sign and pledge of that Sabbath-keeping which remains, the eternal rest of God and of His people, when time shall be no more, and when the redeemed of all ages and dispensations shall enter into full and perfect rest as promised in the word: "There remaineth therefore a sabbath-rest for the people of God" (Heb 4:9, RV).

In an eternity past, before the earth was formed, or the mountains brought forth (Psa 90:2), God - Father, Son, and Spirit - kept Sabbath. After the six days' work as recorded in Genesis 1, again God - Father, Son, and Spirit - rested. The first Sabbath in paradise was the rest of God: "He rested from all His work" which He had "created and made" (Gen 2:3). His creative work was perfect, therefore the operation of His hand ceased and He rested. And as a memorial of His creative power, the seventh day was set apart from the other days of the week.

We have no account of how or in what way it was distinguished and observed before the Fall of man. But the Creator's rest was bound up with the work of which it was the memorial. That work was marred by the entrance of sin and the fall of man from his primal state of innocence. And when Adam fell, his kingdom lost its original perfection. When the work of creation was thus marred, the rest connected with it was broken. The Sabbath could therefore no longer be the memorial of a *present* rest of the Creator in His work. But it was continued as the foreshadowing of another rest, based upon redemption, which in mercy God would introduce, a rest not dependent upon the goodness of the creature, but upon the infinite worth and perfect work of a Redeemer. Thus it was that the Sabbath became a "shadow of Christ", pointing forward to Him who was to come, on whose person and work a new creation was to be framed, and a new rest found, which Satan would be unable to overthrow, or sin to mar.

This was the work spoken of by the Lord Jesus, when He was accused of breaking the Sabbath. "My Father worketh hitherto, and I work" (John 5:17), said the Lord living among men. And before He yielded up His spirit on Calvary, He was able to say triumphantly, "It is finished" (John 19:30). It was to this that Israel's Sabbaths and days of rest pointed; they were the shadows of the rest which was to be found by God and by His people in redemption. The final and complete fulfilment of this Sabbath will be in the eternal rest, in new heavens and a new earth wherein dwelleth righteousness. God's will shall be perfectly done, and God Himself will be all in all.

Even now, however, flowing from the death of Christ, there are and there will be pledges and foretastes of that rest. To the burdened sinner, the Lord Jesus says, "Come unto Me, all ye that labour and are heavy laden, and I will give you rest" (Matt 11:28). And all who hear and obey that call, are even now able to sing,

> "I came to Jesus as I was,
> Weary and worn and sad;
> I found in Him a resting-place,
> And He has made me glad."

To the saint, there is a further and deeper rest, as expressed in the words that follow: "Take My yoke upon you and learn of Me; for I am meek and lowly in heart: and ye shall find rest to your souls" (v.29). This rest is found in obedience to Christ as Lord, in submission to His will, in bowing under His yoke. This is a blessing also to be enjoyed presently.

Also to the servant wearied *in*, but not *of* His Master's work, how sweetly come His words, "Come ye yourselves apart, and rest a while" (Mark 6:31). There, alone a while in the presence of His Master and Lord, away from the bustle and the toil of a busy life, the servant of the Lord is rested and refreshed, and comes forth ready for his toil once again.

To those who have left us and are "with Christ" (Phil 1:23), there has come a further instalment of the promised rest.

Their conflicts are over, their days of toil are ended, and they rest "at home with their Lord" in paradise (see 2 Cor 5:8; Luke 23:43). They "rest from their labours; and their works do follow them" (Rev 14:13).

The millennium will be yet another stage of this God-given rest. During the thousand years of Messiah's reign on earth, Satan will be bound and the groan of creation will cease. The prophetic word will then be fulfilled, "The whole earth is at rest, and is quiet: they break forth into singing" (Isa 14:7). The noise of war, the clash of arms, the cries of the oppressed, the wails of sorrow, will all cease, and under the peaceful beams of the Sun of Righteousness, the benign rule of the Prince of Peace, the wearied earth will keep its Sabbath.

But this, blessed as it is, is not the *final* rest. Sin will lurk beneath the surface. Satan although bound, will not be destroyed. There will be one last great outburst of man's sin and Satan's rage (Rev 20:7), which judgment from heaven will finally quell and end. But after that will come the eternal rest, that unending Sabbath-keeping of God and His people, the rest of eternity which nothing will ever spoil or disturb.

CHAPTER 5

The Passover

"Thou shalt sacrifice the passover at even, at the going down of the sun, at the season that thou camest forth out of Egypt" (Deut 16:6).

"Christ our passover is sacrificed for us: therefore let us keep the feast" (1 Cor 5:7-8).

> *No bone of Thee was broken*
> *Thou spotless Paschal Lamb!*
> *Of life and peace a token,*
> *To us who know Thy Name:*
> *The Head for all the members,*
> *The curse, the vengeance bore,*
> *And God, our God, remembers*
> *His people's sins no more.*

The Passover was the first of Jehovah's set feasts, the first to be instituted (in Exodus 12), and the first in the year. It was observed on the fourteenth day of the first month, the month of Abib (Deut 16:1). It was the great memorial of Israel's redemption by the blood of the lamb, and of their deliverance from Egypt, observed from year to year. We are left in no doubt about its typical meaning, for the Holy Spirit's inspired commentary is "Christ our passover is sacrificed for us" (1 Cor 5:7). The passover (or paschal) Lamb was a type of Christ. Each time it was sacrificed, it pointed onward to Him who was to come, the Lamb of God, through whose atoning death sin was to be put away, and believing sinners brought near to God.

When the Passover was first given to Israel, the people were slaves to Pharaoh, the Egyptian king, and were idolators serving Egypt's gods. They were thus open to the righteous judgment of God. But in mercy that judgment was averted, and they were "passed over". The Divine assurance was given: "When I see the *blood* I will pass over you" (Exod 12:13).

The words, "I will pass over you", are often simply taken to mean the exemption from judgment of those who had sprinkled the blood on their lintel and door-posts; in other words that the judgment passed them by. But the idea is actually much more than that, and even better than that. The verb *pasach (to "pass over"),* occurs in three other passages in the Old Testament, namely, 2 Sam 4:1, 1 Kings 18:21,26, and Isa 31:5. In the last of these references it is the picture of a bird hovering over her young to preserve and protect them from harm. This is how it was on that awful night in Egypt, when the destroyer was sent to execute judgment: it is not only that God spared them; the truth is that He stood on guard at every blood-sprinkled door to protect and preserve them from harm. He became their almighty Saviour. This is the real meaning of the Passover (Reference: *Redemption Truths,* Sir Robert Anderson, ch.2). But it depended on the blood, the blood of the slain lamb. The stroke of judgment had fallen on a spotless victim. The lamb died that they might live. It was when the blood was appropriated, by using the hyssop to sprinkle it on the lintel and side-posts of the door, that immunity from death was secured. The word of Jehovah gave them complete assurance of safety.

The blood of the lamb was thus the foundation of their new relationship to Jehovah, as His people. Redemption by the blood of the lamb was the only thing which gave them any access or title to all the privileges and blessings which they afterwards received and enjoyed as the people of God. The blood was the foundation of everything. The day on which it was shed and sprinkled marked the beginning of their history as Jehovah's redeemed people. It was their birthday as a new and separate nation; their days and months were counted from that day; the entire calendar of their sacred year was made up anew (Exod 12:2).

This shows how redemption and regeneration are always linked together in the thoughts of God. To trust Christ's blood is to be "born again". The six months of the year which had already run their course, were, we might say, blotted out, and then a fresh start was made. Dispensationally, this may point to the period of man's probation, from Adam's fall to the death of Christ. Individually, it shows that at regeneration, the believer ceases to be reckoned any longer as a child of Adam, a fallen sinner. The believer in Christ now stands in Him as a new creation; he begins to live in newness of life. Old things are passed away; his former self is crucified and buried. Now bought *for* God and born *of* God, he goes forth to live for God, no longer to serve sin, the world and Satan. Also, collectively, the church as the body of Christ, and as a habitation of God "in the Spirit", something altogether new, came into existence after the death of Christ upon the cross (Acts 2).

Apart from the death of Christ, and faith in Him who died, apart from the person and work of Christ, there can be no real Christianity on earth, and no title to heaven hereafter. Redemption by blood is the foundation of everything. The cross is the starting-point for the throne. The blood of the

Lamb is our only title to seeing the glory of God. And so from now on Jehovah commanded that the great redemption feast should be kept from year to year (Exod 13:10) throughout their generations. Immediately they had crossed the threshold of their New Year, they were to celebrate this paschal feast. And this was to be continued even after they had reached the land of promise, and had been settled in their inheritance beyond Jordan. The memorial feast was still to be kept (see Josh 5:10 and Deut 16), and when generations to come should ask its meaning, they were to tell to their children the story of their redemption (Exod 12:24-27).

There are many precious details concerning the passover, on which we should delight to meditate. The choice of the lamb, keeping it up from the tenth to the fourteenth day, the manner and time of its death, and the use made of its blood, all have their antitypes in the person and work of Christ who has become our Saviour.

It is worthy of notice, however, that the aspect of the passover presented in Leviticus 23, is not the same as we have in Exodus 12. There, the blood was sprinkled, and the flesh of the lamb roasted with fire and eaten by the Israelites while judgments surrounded them. The cry of anguish was heard on every hand: it was the time of divine judgment. They fed on the roasted lamb, with girded loins and shod feet, ready to depart from Egypt. The passover was there connected with their *salvation* and *separation* to God. But here it is "a feast of Jehovah", to be kept in the peace and rest of their inheritance in Canaan, at the place where Jehovah chose to place His name, while sweet savour offerings ascended from Jehovah's altar to His throne. It was Jehovah's feast, an expression of His own special joy in the great event of which it was a shadow, and His redeemed people were gathered around Him to share that joy in His presence.

What a wonderful thought this is! Jehovah keeping a feast in anticipation of the death of Christ! This surpasses our finite thoughts: we cannot comprehend it! What that death in all its fullness was to Him, no saint or angel can ever know. There were communications between Golgotha and the highest heaven, unknown and unknowable to man. That dying Sufferer was Jehovah's only Son. That obedient, submissive victim was the Lamb of God. That melted, tender heart was the only heart on earth that ever and always beat true to God. Even in the hour of His darkest, deepest woe, He trusted in His God. " He became obedient unto death, even the death of the Cross" (Phil 2:8), and that was in a world where disobedience to God had reigned supreme. That perfect obedience unto death, that complete surrender, that unswerving devotion, was a sweet savour unto God. The cross was a feast to Jehovah. It gave back to Him more than sin had robbed Him of. Yes, blessed be God, there was in the death of God's perfect, spotless Lamb that which satisfied all His desires, fulfilled all His eternal counsels, and brought eternal salvation to all His people.

When we read in the Gospels, we notice how the Lord Jesus honoured the day of the passover by His death. He fulfilled the type in every detail. The lamb was killed in the evening (literally between the two evenings, Exod 12:6, margin), at the going down of the sun (Deut 16:6), as the one day was merging into the next; for the Jewish day is reckoned from sunset to sunset.

So our blessed Lord observed the passover with His disciples in the early hours of the fourteenth day of the month, after sunset. It was night when Judas left the room and when our Lord Jesus instituted the Supper which we keep weekly in remembrance of Him. Later they went out, and the remainder of that night was spent in Gethsemane. "Very early" in the morning He was brought before the Jewish council, hurried from Caiaphas to Pilate, neither of whom could find any fault in Him, the spotless Lamb. Then He was led out to Golgotha. Darkness covered the land from the sixth till the ninth hour, and at the ninth hour, three o'clock in the afternoon, still on the fourteenth day, the Lamb of God died, bearing away the sin of the world.

And thus the Scripture was fulfilled and that great work was done which formed the basis of all God's dealings with man in grace and also in judgment. The plan of the ages was accomplished at Calvary when God's spotless Lamb died. Because of this, the heavens above will be filled with ransomed worshippers, all of whom will own that only the blood of the Lamb brought them there, and all will own it in grateful song. Also, multitudes of the lost in hell, who heard of but despised the great ransom provided, will be made to own and feel that the greatest of all their sins, the fullest measure of their guilt on earth, was that they rejected the Son of God, and despised the value of His atoning blood.

CHAPTER 6

The Feast of Unleavened Bread

"Seven days shalt thou eat unleavened bread therewith, even the bread of affliction" (Deut 16:3).

"Let us keep the feast, not with old leaven, neither with the leaven of malice and wickedness. but with the unleavened bread of sincerity and truth" (1 Cor 5:8, RV).

> *Then within His home he led me,*
> *Brought me where the feast is spread,*
> *Made me eat with Him my Father,*
> *I, who begged for bondsman's bread.*
>
> *Not a suppliant at His gateway,*
> *But a son within His home -*
> *To the love, the joy, the singing,*
> *To the glory I am come.*

The Feast of Unleavened Bread began on the day after the Passover, and continued for seven days - a perfect period of time. The lamb was killed on the fourteenth day, at sunset; the feast of unleavened bread began immediately after the fifteenth day commenced, which was just after sunset, so that there would be no lapse or loss of time, and no interval between the death of the lamb, the sprinkling of the blood, and the keeping of this feast.

It was like this when the feast was first kept in the land of Egypt. The lamb was slain in the evening, the judgment fell at midnight, and the redeemed people of the Lord were out of Egypt in the morning. The killing of the lamb was a single act, and the Passover was reckoned as a one-day feast, as was also the Feast of First-fruits, Pentecost, and the Atonement. These one-day feasts all point to certain great acts of Jehovah's hand, certain definite transactions of His, perfect and complete in themselves. But those feasts which were of seven or eight-day continuance, point to the outcome of these acts, and their results in blessing to the people of God.

Thus, the Passover is the type of Christ's death and shows how God was satisfied with it once for all; then the seven-day feast of unleavened bread points to the outcome of it in the whole course and character of the believer's life on earth, from the day of his conversion onward. It speaks of our communion with God based upon redemption, in holiness and truth. The blood of Christ is the foundation of all true fellowship with God. The person of Christ, our feeding on the Lamb slain, is the only means whereby such fellowship may be maintained. Holiness, the putting away of leaven, is the condition necessary for its enjoyment. We have the Holy Spirit's own exposition of all this fully given in 1 Corinthians 5:7-8: "Christ our passover is sacrificed for us: therefore let us keep the feast not with old leaven, neither with the leaven of malice and wickedness; but with the unleavened bread of sincerity and truth".

The blood on the door-posts and lintel was the foundation of everything; not only of security, but also of peace. There could have been no peaceful feeding on the lamb, no assurance of safety apart from it. So there cannot be true communion with God until there is knowledge of salvation and settled peace with God. When this had been made secure, then the lamb roast with fire was placed on the table, and around it the redeemed of the Lord gathered to keep the feast. What a precious feast for the ransomed soul is the person of Christ, the Lamb of God sacrificed! the Holy One of God slain for sinners! To feed on Him gives strength for what lies ahead.

Girded loins, shod feet, and staff in hand, all speak of pilgrimage. The Israelites stood in Egypt, but they did not belong to it. They were ready to go at the signal from heaven. So also the saints of God today are pilgrims here. The world is not our home - see 1 Peter 2:11. The cross of Christ has detached us from it, cutting all the links that had bound us to it, and has made us strangers here. One has written -

> "The cords that bound my heart to earth
> Were loosed by Jesus' hand;
> Before His Cross I found myself
> A stranger in the land."

The keeping of the feast in Egypt, in the wilderness, and in Canaan, in the place where the Lord would put His name, was always to have the same character throughout. The people's surroundings were different, but the feast remained the same. Redemption as the basis of communion is unchangeable. Whether as "strangers" in the world ready to depart, as in Exodus 12:2; or "pilgrims" in the wilderness passing onward, as in Numbers 9:1-3; or "possessors" of the land of promise, as in Joshua 5:10 - the feast was just the same. Thus we learn that the saint's communion is first based on redemption, then it is sustained by feeding on Christ, and it is maintained in holiness and separation from evil. These are principles of eternal value, unchangeable as the character of God.

The feast was to be kept with "unleavened bread", and no leaven, or leavened bread was to be seen in the Israelites' habitations. It is worthy of notice, how strict and how searching were the commandments of Jehovah concerning leaven and its use: (i) no leavened bread was to be eaten; (ii) no leaven was to be seen; (iii) no leaven was to be allowed in their houses (Exod 13:7). The most diligent search had to be made in the cupboard and the kneading-trough, to make sure that no particle of the corrupt thing was there, or else "a little leaven" left and allowed, would soon leaven "the whole lump" (1 Cor 5:6).

Throughout the Bible, leaven is the figure of evil; only evil, always evil, and of such evil as permeates and carries corruption with it wherever it works. There must be none of this allowed where communion with God is sought. There always will be sin in our nature, but sin in practice, sin as it appears in its workings, must not be allowed, or else communion with a holy God is impossible. "Put off the old man"; "Put away lying"; "Lay aside all malice" (Eph 4:22,25; 1 Pet 2:1) - are words that show what God means by the putting away of leaven, by those who would commune with God. "Old leaven" may refer to old habits, old sins, and old associations, indulged and loved before conversion. These, especially in moments of unwatchfulness, are apt to assert their power, and lead the believer into captivity. It is well to remember that the roots of every sin man was ever guilty of, still remain in the flesh, and but for the restraining grace of God and the indwelling Spirit, they would yield their fruit. But if this is what is meant by old leaven, what then can "new leaven" be? It reminds us that there are other forms of evil to which believers are subject which also may spoil their communion with God, if they become unwatchful and neglectful of self-judgment, just as readily as the sins of their unregenerate days would surely do. There can be envy, jealousy, pride, boasting, conceit in spiritual things, a sectarian spirit, a desire to be important or uppermost, and a host of kindred sins to which the unconverted are not exposed. Satan often uses these in believers, for evil and corruption in a way that he cannot use them in the world. These, and all that leads up to them, must be judged and put away in the individual saint, and in the assembly of saints, if communion with God is to be maintained.

Unleavened bread was to be eaten seven days. "The unleavened bread of *sincerity* and *truth*" is the New Testament answer to this part of the type. Here we have the positive side of what we are considering. The putting away of leaven is the negative side; eating "unleavened bread" is the positive side, and it is important to attend to both. One-sided leaning, either one way or the other, is dangerous, and when pressed too far is disastrous. In our spiritual lives, a true balance has to be kept in everything for our safety.

What is "*sincerity*"? A "sincere" man is usually taken to mean an earnest, well-meaning person, who does what he believes to be right, even if his judgment is far wrong. This word, however, is used in Philippians 1:10 and it has a deeper meaning: it means "pure when viewed in the sunlight" - just as you would take a drop of water and hold it on your finger between you and the sun. It is all clear; there is no impurity in it. "Sincerity" implies that there has been a holding of ourselves and our ways up to the light of God, a continual judging of all our motives, ways, and works in God's sunlight. No doubt this will often show what is not "pure in the sunlight", and will cause us to bow our hearts in confession, and our heads in shame before Him. Yet this is His way, and it is the way of holiness and health to our souls. It gives relish to the feast. Never does the soul so enjoy Christ as when self-judged.

Being in "the sunlight" before God, leads always to the cross and to the person of Christ. "The bread of affliction" (Deut 16:3) forms part of the feast all the way through life's journey.

"And *truth*": this too forms part of the feast. Truthfulness must mark the people of God or there can be no real communion with each other or with God, as we read, "Speak every man truth with his neighbour" (Eph 4:25). But also the truth of God must have its place in our hearts and lives, His whole counsel; no part kept back, no part neglected, nothing exaggerated out of measure. "The communion of saints" is perhaps a subject much spoken of but little known. But when we live in sincerity and in truth, this communion, first with our God and next with our brethren, will be sustained and continued through the "seven days" of our earthly life, right on to that hour, when the resurrection morning shall break. Then those on earth who wake and watch, together with all the saints who have fallen asleep, will be introduced to the unbroken communion of the feast above. There the Lamb in the midst of the throne shall still and ever be the subject of their worship and the subject of their praise, surrounded by hosts in heaven who continually proclaim Him thrice holy and for ever worthy.

CHAPTER 7

The Feast of Firstfruits

"The first of the firstfruits of thy land thou shalt bring into the house of the Lord thy God" (Exod 23:19).

"Now is Christ risen from the dead and become the firstfruits of them that slept" (1 Cor 15:20).

> First-fruits of the resurrection,
> He is risen from the tomb,
> Now I stand in new creation,
> Free because beyond my doom.

Closely connected with the Passover, and while the Feast of Unleavened Bread was in progress, the third of Jehovah's Feasts took place - the Feast of First-fruits. It, however, was to be celebrated in the land of Canaan. Israel had observed the Passover and the Feast of Unleavened Bread during the years of their journey through the wilderness (see Numbers 9:2-5), but before they could celebrate the Feast of Firstfruits, or indeed any of the feasts that followed it, they would have to become possessors of the land of promise.

Their calling and their destiny was not the wilderness, but the land. They had to pass through the wilderness, and learn its lessons (Deut 8:3), but it was not to be their dwelling place. The purpose of Jehovah, who had brought them out of Egypt by His outstreched arm of power, was to bring them into the goodly land of Canaan flowing with milk and honey, "a land of wheat and barley, and vines, and fig-trees, and pomegranates" (Deut 8:7-9), where they should lack nothing.

Once they had come into that land of fullness and experienced for themselves the goodness of God, this new ordinance of the sheaf of first-fruits was to be observed. In the midst of prosperity, the claims of Jehovah were to be first remembered. "Ye shall eat neither bread, nor parched corn, nor green ears, until the selfsame day that ye have brought an offering unto your God" (Lev 23:14). That offering was a sheaf reaped from the waving fields of ripened harvest, and carried to the priest, to be waved before the Lord to be accepted for them, followed by burnt-offering, meat-offering, and drink-offering (notably, no sin-offering). The time when this was to be done was "the day after the Sabbath".

After the journey through the wilderness was over and the river Jordan crossed, after Israel settled in the land of promise, they offered the sheaf of first-fruits, and reaped their harvests year after year. But they did not understood the meaning of this ordinance, any more than they understood the killing of the paschal lamb, although both were foreshadowings of Christ. Another Lamb, another First-fruits, and other harvests, were in the mind of God. And when the fullness of the time had come (Gal 4:4) for the great antitype of these to be revealed among men, the nation of Israel ought to have discerned and received Him with joy. But sin and unbelief had blinded their eyes. They saw no beauty in the Lamb of God when He was presented to them; they led Him out to the slaughter. Neither did they own and receive Him after He, as the First-fruits, had risen from the dead. Instead they forged a lie in the face of His empty grave, and sought to stifle the voices of His servants who preached His resurrection from among the dead. Because of this, Israel's harvests of blessing lie still unreaped, and the great Husbandman has gone forth to other fields which, like Samaria was in the days of the Lord's earthly ministry, are "white unto harvest" (John 4:35).

There can be no doubt that the sheaf of first-fruits reaped from the harvest field on the morrow after the Sabbath, the pledge to Israel of many sheaves to follow, and waved before Jehovah in His temple for acceptance, was a type and foreshadowing of *Christ risen from the dead*. The name of that sheaf is very the name given to Him as the One risen from among the dead - "Christ the First-fruits". And then, as if to show the close connection of that sheaf with the harvest to follow, the Spirit adds - "afterwards, they that are Christ's at His coming" (1 Cor 15:23).

The Lord Jesus honoured the day of the killing of the paschal lamb by presenting Himself to God in death, "a Lamb without blemish and without spot". He honoured the day of the waving of the sheaf of first-fruits by presenting Himself to God as the First-born from among the dead. Israel's priest no doubt that day waved the sheaf before a rent veil in the temple at Jerusalem; but outside that city's gates God had reaped the great Wave-sheaf from Joseph's tomb early that same morning. The substance had come, and the shadow passed away. "When the Sabbath was past" (Mark 16:1), and the Marys had gone out "very early in the morning" to the tomb, they found it empty. The Lord had risen. The first great sheaf had been reaped of that harvest which God has since been gathering into the garners of heaven. All these will be accepted in and associated with their great representative, the "First-born" from among the dead.

Here we might pause for a moment and refresh our spirits by a brief survey of this great fact, the resurrection of our Lord Jesus Christ, and what it involves for Him, and for us. Even now the saints are "quickened together with Christ"

(Eph 2:5), they share His life, they are risen with Him (Col 3:1). In incarnation, He was the only-begotten Son of God (John 1:14; 3:16), and as such He stood alone. It has been erroneously taught, that in becoming man, He linked Himself with our race, and this raised men as men to a higher level and to acceptance by God. The Scriptures do not teach this at all. They clearly and definitely teach that only by redemption and regeneration are sinners brought from death to life, and from Satan to God. This is the only way of vital union with Christ. "Union in Incarnation" and the "Common Fatherhood of God" preached by many, ignore the clear words of the Lord Jesus, "Ye must be born again" (John 3:7).

As "the corn of wheat" He also stood alone in His death, the only begotten of the Father; but having died, He arose, no longer alone, but as "the First-born from the dead" (Col 1:18), "the First-born among many brethren" (Rom 8:29). This new relationship was first made known to Mary on the resurrection morning, in those ever-memorable words of the risen Christ in the garden, "I ascend to My Father and your Father, to My God and your God" (John 20:17). Just as the acceptance of the sheaf of first-fruits presented before Jehovah was for the whole of Israel's harvest, so the acceptance and welcome to heaven given to Christ as the representative of all His people, is the seal and the pledge of their welcome there. Even now they stand in His acceptance; they are "accepted in the Beloved" (Eph 1:6). The Father's love to Him is the measure of the Father's love to them (John 17:23). They are as near and dear to God as Christ is. What a wonderful truth! Well may we sing -

> *So dear, so very dear to God,*
> *More dear I cannot be;*
> *The love wherewith He loves the Son,*
> *Such is His love to me.*

This is the present sphere of blessing to which the resurrection of Christ introduces His people. But what about the future? The resurrection of the dead (Heb 6:2), is one of the great foundation truths of Scripture. It was denied by the Sadducees (Matt 22:23), as it is now by modern rationalists and atheists. Since the day that the Jewish elders "gave large money" to the Roman guard to circulate the lie that the disciples of the Lord stole His dead body from the tomb while they were asleep, there has been a succession of attempts made by "enemies of the Cross" to deny the resurrection. The devil does not like it to be known that although he put forth all his power to crush the Son of God at Calvary and to hold His body in the grave, he was utterly defeated in the former, and completely routed in the latter attempt. Wincing under this humiliation, and enraged at the exaltation of the Prince of Life to the throne in the heavens, the Adversary gives his chief attention to attacking all that God has written concerning the glories and triumphs of His Son. Need we wonder that Christ's resurrection, in which He was "declared to be the Son of God with power" (Rom 1:4), is a chief object of his hate. In early times, there were rationalists who scoffed at it (1 Cor 15:35). Others nowadays deny it on other grounds, making it mythical and symbolic or spiritual, with the result that "Jesus and the resurrection" (Acts 17:18) is little heard of in popular preaching.

It was generally accepted among the Jews that there would be a "resurrection of the dead" (Acts 23:6). Martha of Bethany's words to the Lord concerning her brother Lazarus, aptly express the Jewish faith on the subject, "I know that he shall rise again in the resurrection at the last day" (John 11:24). This was all the light that had been given, but the Lord's answer in v.25, tells of something brighter and better. Once and again he had hinted to His disciples that there would be a resurrection "*from* (literally *from among)* the dead" (Mark 9:9-10, see Newberry, Rotherham, etc.), but they did not grasp the meaning of His words. The resurrection *of* the dead is true of all; all who have died, whether saved or lost, shall be raised, though not at the same time or for the same destiny. There will be a "resurrection of life" and a "resurrection of judgment" (John 5:29), a "resurrection of the just and the unjust" (Acts 24:15). The resurrection of the Lord Jesus was "from among the dead", and this is the word that is always used to describe the resurrection of His people. It will be an "out-resurrection" (Phil 3:11, Newberry); a resurrection "from among dead ones". When the Lord shall descend from heaven with a shout, "the dead in Christ shall rise first" (1 Thess 4:16). But the unconverted dead in the graves around them will not stir on that fair morning. When the great First-fruit Sheaf Himself was reaped, we read that "many bodies of the saints" that had fallen asleep were raised, and *after* His resurrection appeared (Matt 27:15), a pledge of the greater harvest still to come; but not one sinner's tomb was stirred, not one of the unregenerate arose. So shall it be at the first resurrection. "The rest of the dead" live not again, until the thousand years of millennial blessedness have passed (Rev 20:5), and then they are raised for judgment (Rev 20:12). How vast the difference both in time and character is their resurrection from that of Christ and His saints!

There were sweet-savour sacrifices offered on the same day as the sheaf was waved at this feast which we have been considering. These may point to the basis of our association with, and our acceptance in, the risen Christ. He ascended to heaven in the excellency of His own peerless Person; but *our* title to be there with Him, now by faith, and soon in bodily presence, is found only in the worth of the one great sacrifice offered for us. Even when we stand in resurrection bodies among the glories of heaven, our song shall be then as it is now of the Lamb who was slain for us:

> *I stand upon His merit,*
> *I know no other stand;*
> *Not e'en where glory dwelleth*
> *In Immanuel's land.*

CHAPTER 8

Pentecost, the Feast of Weeks

"Thou shalt keep the feast of weeks unto the Lord thy God, with a tribute of a free-will offering of thine hand, which thou shalt give unto the Lord thy God" (Deut 16:10).

"When the day of Pentecost was fully come, they were all together in one place" (Acts 2:1).

"Ye are all one in Christ Jesus" (Gal 3:28).

> *O teach us, Lord, to know and own*
> *This wondrous mystery;*
> *That Thou with us art truly one,*
> *And we are one with Thee.*

Fifty days after the wave-sheaf had been reaped and presented before God, the redeemed people were again gathered to the place where Jehovah had placed His name. This was to celebrate the Feast of Weeks, or Pentecost. The former of these names is derived from the fact that the celebration of this feast was seven weeks or a week of weeks after the feast of Firstfruits. The latter name, Pentecost. describes the same period in days, the Greek word *pentecost* meaning the fiftieth.

The services of the Feast of Weeks consisted in a new meat-offering being offered before the Lord. This meat-offering was to be two loaves of fine flour, fruit of the new harvest which had just been gathered in, baked "with leaven", then waved before the Lord by the priest, accompanied by sweet savour offerings and sin offerings. There is a striking similarity and a close connection between this feast and the feast of First-fruits. They are introduced in Leviticus 23:9 by the usual introductory words, "And the Lord spake unto Moses, saying", and these words do not again occur till v.23, where the Feast of Trumpets is introduced. Thus, just as the Passover and the Feast of Unleavened Bread are associated together, so too are the Feast of Firstfruits and Pentecost.

We have already seen that the answer to the Passover has been found in the death of Christ, and that the First-fruits has had its fulfilment in His resurrection from among the dead. We have now to enquire whether there has been a fulfilment of Pentecost, and if so, what that fulfilment is. We do not have to search far to find it. The antitype of this feast is found in the descent of the Holy Spirit, described in Acts 2, and the formation of the church, composed of all believers, Jews and Gentiles alike, to make "one new man" (Eph 2:15).

We have already observed that our Lord Jesus honoured the day of the Passover by His death, and that God the Father honoured the day of the First-fruits by raising up Christ from among the dead as the firstfruits of a glorious harvest. So we now find that the Holy Spirit honoured the feast of Pentecost by His descent upon the waiting and expectant disciples, who were found gathered together waiting for the promised Comforter when that very day was "being fulfilled" (Acts 2:1, RV). On these waiting souls the Spirit descended, uniting them into one body (1 Cor 12:13), filling each one, and filling the whole house in which they were assembled. This was the inauguration of a new work of God's grace among men, such as had not been seen in all the ages that had gone before. What are the special characteristics of this work? Let us turn to our type in Leviticus 23, and examine its various parts in the light of New Testament scripture.

The Feast of Firstfruits pointed to the risen Christ accepted for His people within the heavens. Now the loaves of Pentecost are also called "firstfruits unto the Lord" (Lev 23:17). This identifies them with the wave-sheaf. It was the precursor of the harvest. The loaves were made of flour, from the same crop as that sheaf. They were of the same grain, reaped from the same field, but the wave-sheaf was pre-eminent over everything else. So it is with Christ and His believing people. He is "the Firstfruits" (1 Cor 15:20); then of the saints it is written, "Of His own will begat He us with the Word of Truth, that we should he a kind of firstfruits of His creatures" (James 1:18). He is the "Firstborn among many brethren" (Rom 8:29) - "the Sanctifier and the sanctified are all of one" (Heb 2:11). We make up the "church of the firstborn which are written in heaven" (Heb 12:23).

Now this is a glorious truth to be received into the heart in all its unction and blessing. What a power it brings with it to the soul! What a horizon it opens up to the spiritual vision! We are one with Christ; in our standing before God in Christ, accepted, complete, filled full. We are no more in fallen Adam of the earth; but in the second Man, the last Adam, Christ risen and ascended to heaven. This is the place of every believer; God has given it to all His people. How few believe it, and how little do any of us really enjoy it! Yet there it is, given us by our God to be apprehended, received, and enjoyed from day to day. How is this to be? By the indwelling Holy Spirit, given to each believer. He is a witness of the exaltation of Christ (Heb 10:15; Acts 2:32-33). "The *firstfruits* of the Spirit" (Rom 8:23), given to all believers, is the seal of their oneness with Christ (Eph 1:13), the earnest and pledge of their resurrection, and association with Him in glory, and the power for enjoyment of this great truth on earth. Apart from Christ's glorification at God's right hand, the Spirit would not have come down to indwell believers (John 16:7). His presence in and with them, is the witness that Christ is accepted at the right hand of God (John

15:26). The presence of the Holy Spirit on earth, and the union of believers with the risen Christ at God's right hand by the Spirit, are the two great characteristics of this present age or day of grace.

The two loaves point to the fact that God is gathering out from Jew and Gentile, a people for Himself. Before Pentecost, these two peoples were divided by a "middle wall of partition" (Eph 2:14). The Jews were the chosen seed. To them pertained "the adoption, and the glory, and the covenants" (Rom 9:14). "Unto them were committed the oracles of God" (Rom 3:2). The Gentiles, however, were aliens and strangers, afar off, and without God (Eph 2:12). Both had shown themselves against Christ, and in that memorable prayer offered to God, when such opposition to God's grace had been shown in Jerusalem, these words were uttered, "Against thy holy servant Jesus, whom Thou didst anoint, both Herod and Pontius Pilate, with the *Gentiles,* and the *peoples of Israel* were gathered together" (Acts 4:27, RV). God had concluded there was "no difference" between them (Rom 3:22). The cross had manifested their common guilt and hatred of Christ. It had also broken down the middle wall of partition that divided them. Now, by the descent of the Holy Spirit, the two, that is believing Jews and believing Gentiles, were formed into "one new man" (Eph 2:15*).* The cross reconciled *both* in one body to God, and in one Spirit *both* have access to the Father (Eph 2:16-18, RV).

This great work was inaugurated by the descent of the Spirit on the day of Pentecost, and here it is beautifully set forth in type, by the two wave-loaves being presented together as one before the Lord. This was the mystery "hid in God", which had not been made known in former ages, "that the Gentiles are fellow-heirs, and fellow-members of the body, and fellow-partakers of the promise in Christ Jesus" (Eph 3:6, RV); and it is written, "in one Spirit were we all baptised into one body, whether Jews or Greeks, whether bond or free, and were all made to drink of one Spirit (1 Cor 12:13, RV). This is the unique and privileged place given to the saints of this age, to all saints of every nation, from Pentecost till the coming of the Lord to the air to call His people away from earth to heaven. It is the special calling and portion of the church, the body of Christ, in contrast to everything which had gone before and that will follow after. It might be summed up as having union with Christ the Head in heaven, and with all His saints by the Holy Spirit. Truly, "this is the Lord's doing, and it is marvellous in our eyes". Also remember that being the workmanship of God, the church thus formed is indissolubly and eternally one. Men can neither mar it nor mutilate it. Its unity is divinely created and divinely sustained, so that the gates of hell shall never prevail against it. Such is the church viewed in its heavenly and divine relationship to Christ, begun at Pentecost by the descent of the Spirit, now being gathered and fashioned by the Lord, and which, when completed, will be raised and presented to God in all the perfectness of Christ.

The two wave-loaves point also to another aspect of the church, namely that which is earthly and visible as well as what is heavenly and unseen. It first appeared among men on that Pentecost-day and the days that followed. On that day there was brought into existence a united company of believers, of one heart and soul, found together and manifesting before men their common interests in Christ and in each other. This was a heavenly people in mortal flesh on earth, indwelt by the heaven-sent Spirit, manifesting His fruits, and standing forth in His power before the eyes of men. It was to this company that the name of "the church" (Acts 5:11; 8:1) was first given. It was chiefly or wholly composed of believing Jews to begin with, but in process of time the gospel reached the Gentiles through Peter's lips, who had been chosen as the instrument to open the door of faith to the Jews first, and afterwards to the Gentiles (see Matt 16:18; Acts 2:14, with 15:7). Others were brought into this "one flock" (John 10:16), and thus believing Gentiles became manifestly associated with believing Jews, and together formed the "churches of God in Christ Jesus" (1 Thess 2:14) wherever found.

Although at first slowly owned by believing Jews, and even by Peter himself (Acts 10:28; 11:3-18), this was the earthly answer to the heavenly pattern, and was afterwards more fully made known to and by the apostle Paul, "the wise master-builder" (1 Cor 3:10). To him, by revelation, was committed the full pattern of the church's constitution, fellowship, ordinances, ministry, and rule; and in his epistles, he has passed the same on to us and to all saints of this age (see 1 Cor 11-14; 1 Tim 3:1-16). This divine legislation for the church as given in the Word continues through the entire age, and God has neither repealed it nor added to it since it was given. Happy had it been for all the saints, had they received and always acted on it, and not been influenced by the traditions and commandments of men.

The two wave-loaves were baked "with leaven". Leaven is always and everywhere the type of corruption. There was no leaven in the meat-offering (Lev 2:11), because that offering is a type of the perfect manhood and character of Christ Himself. He was intrinsically holy in His character and ways. But this is not so with His people. Even after conversion and with the Spirit dwelling within, the believer is not personally free from corruption. The flesh is still within him: the presence of the Spirit does not expel or alter it, although by grace its power is no longer dominant. It is restrained, but not eradicated, hence the believer is not sinless. He is not as was Jesus Christ his Lord, fit to be placed on the altar for divine acceptance, for atoning and meritorious sacrifice. Hence we read that with, or over the wave-loaves, sin-offering and sweet-savour offerings were presented for their acceptance. The two loaves were thus presented to Jehovah, with leaven in them, but they were under the shelter and covered with the preciousness of these other offerings. So it is that believers individually, and the church collectively stand as a new meat-offering before God, accepted in all the value of Christ's peerless person and atoning work. The moment that either individual Christians, or God's churches on earth, begin to think that personal devotion or service gives acceptance before God; or that any measure of obedience to the truth gives merit in His sight; or that gifts and graces eradicate the corruption that dwells within – they will find out sooner or later that they have been deceived by Satan.

The church even in its early beauty and freshness had the leaven within it, and soon in varied aspects it began to manifest itself, both in doctrine and in practice. It was found in the church at Jerusalem (Acts 5:1; 15:1), the churches at Galatia (Gal. 5:9), and the church of God at Corinth (1 Cor. 5:6-7). In these last days in which we live, new and unheard of departures from the faith are being multiplied, doctrines of demons pour forth on every hand, and evil men and seducers wax worse and worse. This appearance of leaven in its various forms need not alarm us, although it should always humble us. It should send us to seek again the rest of our souls individually, and collectively as God's church, in the peerless person and ever-precious work of Christ, the only foundation on which we stand, sanctified in Christ Jesus (1 Cor 1:2), to be the Spirit's holy temple in the Lord (Eph 2:21-22).

His precious blood is all my plea,
My only title there;
Himself my costly offering,
Unblemished pure and rare.

CHAPTER 9

The Present Interval

"God did visit the Gentiles to take out of them a people for His name" (Acts 15:14).

"Blindness in part is happened to Israel, until the fulness of the Gentiles be come in" (Rom 11:25).

> *His chosen Bride, ordained with Him,*
> *To reign o'er all the earth*
> *Must first be formed, ere Israel know*
> *Her Saviour's matchless worth.*

Up till now in our study of the Feasts of Jehovah we have considered four of the seven feasts described in Leviticus 23. These four were all linked together in the time of their observation within the first three months of the calendar, and in their sequence as each followed on from the one before it. In fact the times of their celebration were all calculated from the first, the Passover on the fourteenth day of the first month. All Israel's national blessings began with that, as ours all begin at the cross of our Lord Jesus Christ. We have noted too that the great events to which these feasts pointed - the death, burial, and resurrection of Christ, and the descent of the Holy Spirit to form and indwell the church - these are also inseparably linked together. Now after the Feast of Weeks there is a long period of fully four months before the next feast, the Feast of Trumpets which would take place on the first day of the seventh month. Reference to the chart at the back of this book showing the seven feasts will confirm this.

During these four months of the year the harvest of the fields and the vintage of the vineyards were gathered in. There was no holy convocation of the people during these busy months, no fresh subject of interest was introduced to occupy their thoughts. They reaped the fruits of that goodly land which Jehovah had given to them, and on which His eye and heart were ever resting. This interval was important for them, and we shall see how important it is to us, for it represents this present age of grace in which we live, and the work that God is doing throughout its course.

On the day of Pentecost when the Spirit of God descended, God began gathering out from all the nations a people to form the church, the body of Christ. Since then there has been no new operation of God's hand among men. The work of proclaiming the gospel among all nations, and the discipling of them (Matt 28:19), has been going on continuously. The dispensation then inaugurated, continues still, and that mystic body, of which all the members were written in God's book before the foundation of the world (Eph 1:4), is still "in continuance being fashioned" (Psa 139:16) under the hand of the Holy Spirit. This work will continue until the advent of the Son of God from heaven. The dispensation that now runs its course began at the descent of the Spirit, and it will end at the descent of the Son, and the consequent ascent of the saints to heaven. If we remember this simple fact we will be preserved from many errors about present fulfilments of prophecy regarding God's earthly people Israel, and from trying to apply Scriptures to the events of the present period which can only have their fulfilment in a future age after the call of the church is complete.

As regards Israel, God's direct dealings with them are at present broken off, "until the fulness of the Gentiles" has been gathered in (Rom 11:25). This means that no prophecy concerning their full restoration and future glory can possibly be fulfilled while the present dispensation runs its course. But after the work of calling and ingathering the church has been completed, God will turn His heart and hand to His earthly people once again. And then "times and seasons" (Acts 1:7), and the threads of God's promise and prophecy towards His earthly people, will be taken up again just where they were broken off. Then prophetic dates will again resume their course. During the present age, believing Jews are being incorporated into the church, the body of Christ, but they are few in number, just as the "gleanings of the corners of the harvest-field" (Lev 23:22), a feeble "remnant according to the election of grace" (Rom 11:5). But when the Lord puts forth His hand to recover and regather His earthly people as a nation, it will not be by means of the gospel as now preached among the nations, but by other agencies and with more wide-spread results.

It is worth repeating that although the national sin of Israel has postponed the fulfilment of the promises made to the fathers, it has not blotted them out, nor caused the faithfulness of God to fail. Even though that sin culminated in the crucifixion of their Messiah (Acts 2:23), and in the rejection of the Holy Spirit's testimony to Him as glorified in the heavens (Acts 7:56), God in His mercy will take them up again. The chapters telling of Israel's present unbelief and off-cutting (Rom 9-11) do not close without the assurance that, in spite of their sin, they shall yet be visited in mercy. "For," says the inspired writer, "the gifts and calling of God are not repented of" (11:29, RV). Christendom in its pride may have despised the Jew, and even appropriated to itself promises of earthly blessing, for example writing above such passages as Isaiah 11 and 32, "Promises to the Church", and "Blessings of the Gospel" (as in some Bible headlines), but they belong by right to the restored and regenerated earthly people, when in the latter day they turn to the Lord.

There is no indication here or anywhere else in Scripture, that the present dispensation will run its course until the end of time, or that the world will be converted by the gospel as now proclaimed among men. The Lord will accomplish His purpose in the gathering of His earthly people, and the subjugation of the world to its rightful King, in another way. What that way is, our study of the three remaining feasts of this prophetic chapter will show.

Before going on, it is worth noting that these three feasts, which all took place in the seventh month and followed each other in quick succession, have a double meaning. They have a heavenly and an earthly fulfilment, that is, their antitypes and answers will be found in events yet to take place in the heavens and in the earth as recorded in the Word of God. In days to come, the operations of the divine hand will proceed simultaneously towards those who share the heavenly calling and belong to heaven, and likewise towards the earthly people who will again be in covenant relationship with Jehovah. The heavens and the earth will not then be separated by sin, as they are now, but united in one, for "in that day there shall be one Lord and His name one" (Zech 14:9), and unto Him shall the gathering of the people be. The same glorified Lord will be the Head of the church, the King of Israel and the Lord of all creation. He will be honoured by all in the heavens above and all in the earth beneath, and men of every nation, people, and tongue, will unite to own Jesus of Nazareth "Lord of all".

To Thee the world its treasure brings,
To Thee the mighty bow;
To Thee the Church exulting sings,
Her Sovereign-Saviour Thou!

CHAPTER 10

The Feast of Trumpets

"The trumpet shall sound ; and the dead shall be raised incorruptible, and we shall be changed" (1 Cor 15:52).

"He shalt send His angels with a great sound of a trumpet, and they shall gather together His elect" (Matt 24:31).

> *Hark to the trump! behold it breaks*
> *The sleep of ages now,*
> *And lo! the light of glory shines*
> *On many an aching brow.*
>
> *The scattered sons of Israel's race,*
> *That trumpet's sound shall bring*
> *Back to their land: to know and own*
> *Messiah as their King.*

The Feast of Trumpets, which was observed on the first day of the seventh month, begins the second series of "Jehovah's set feasts", and it was quickly followed by the Day of Atonement, and the Feast of Tabernacles. As has been already indicated, these feasts all point forward to great events of the future which God will yet bring to pass, for both His heavenly and His earthly people. In the days that are to come, He will glorify and exalt His Christ in the heavens above and in the earth beneath, and gather together in one under Him, things celestial and things terrestrial (Eph 1:10).

The blowing of trumpets was an ancient ordinance in Israel. In their wilderness days, two silver trumpets made from the atonement money of the people, were blown "for the calling of the assembly, and for the journeyings of the camps" (Num 10:2). In days of gladness, and in times of war, the blast of the trumpet was a familiar sound among the tribes of Israel. It was the voice of Jehovah their Redeemer, who had brought them out from Egypt to be a special people unto Himself. All His commandments were given on the ground of redemption, and as His redeemed people, He claimed their obedience. The application of this to the saints of today is plain enough. The Lord's people are a purchased people, "a people for His own possession" (Titus 2:14, RV), redeemed from all lawlessness; no longer their own, but bought with a price to glorify God (1 Cor 6:20), and as obedient children to do His will.

"His commandments are not grievous" (1 John 5:3), difficult to understand or to obey. They fall on the ear of His people as the words of their Redeemer, and when constrained by love to Him, they swiftly and willingly obey. It was of such obedience that the Psalmist sang, "Blessed is the people that know the *trumpet sound:* they walk O Lord, in the light of Thy countenance" (Psa 89:15, RV). And thus it is that communion with God is sustained, by loving, loyal, hearty, uncompromising obedience to every word that comes to us from Him who has redeemed us. This even now, in the wilderness days of the saints, is as a feast to God which, as in days of old, He comes to share (Gen 18:1-18) with His obedient people (John 14:23) and they with Him (Rev 3:20).

But the full answer to the Feast of Trumpets is yet to come, and will have its grand fulfilment in that wonderful coming day when "the Lord Himself shall descend from heaven with a shout, with the voice of the archangel and with the trump of God" (1 Thess 4:16). At "the last trump" (1 Cor 15:52), the dead in Christ shall be raised incorruptible, having put on incorruptibility, and the living will be changed, having put on immortality. Both will together rise to meet their Lord in the air, the One who has come to receive them unto Himself, as He promised He would.

> Him eye to eye we then shall see,
> Our face like His shall shine;
> O what a glorious company
> When saints and angels join.

What joy and triumph filled the hearts of the children of Israel in ancient days when they gathered to the city of the great King, as the blast of the silver trumpet rang out through all their land! But what will it be when "the last trump" shall sound, and every one of the redeemed shall rise to meet their Lord in the air? Who can describe or conceive the bliss of that moment ? What a triumph over death! The graves emptied of all the ransomed dead! The world cleared of all the living saints, and all gathered in resurrection beauty to their home above!

> Ascending through the crowded air,
> On eagle wings they soar
> To dwell in the full joy of love,
> And sorrow there no more.

This Feast of Trumpets will also have its fulfilment in the awakening and gathering of God's earthly people Israel. For long centuries they have been as in the slumber of death, a people scattered throughout the world, but the "set time" to favour Zion (Psa 102:13) will come. The prophetic Scriptures of the Old Testament teem with glowing words describing this event, when the trumpet shall be blown in Zion (Psa 81:3), and the long-lost and scattered people shall flock around their once rejected Lord and King. The Lord Himself spoke of this after He had wept over Jerusalem, which had refused to be gathered under His sheltering wing (Matt 23:37). Looking far onward to the time of the end, He told them they should "see the Son of Man coming in the clouds of heaven, with power and great glory. And He shall send His angels with a sound of a great trumpet, and they shall gather His elect from the four winds, from the one end of heaven to the other" (24:30, 31).

This refers to the earthly people, Israel, being gathered to their land, at the coming of the Son of Man to earth, whereas the heavenly people are to be gathered around Him, when, at an earlier period He descends to the air as Son of God. In the heavens above, these saints see His face without a veil or a cloud between, and they bask in the light of His countenance. On the earth, the "outcasts of Israel and the dispersed of Judah", the earthly people, as those "ready to perish" (Isa 27:13), will be gathered one by one from distant lands and islands to Immanuel's land, the land promised to Israel as long ago as the time of Abraham (Gen 13:15).

This gathering must not be confused with an earlier return of a part of the people of Israel to their land in unbelief, when they will enter into a covenant with Antichrist only to be deceived (see Daniel 9:27), and persecuted in the Great Tribulation of which the Lord Jesus spoke (Matt 24:21). This is rather what is described by the prophet Zechariah when he writes of a repentant and mourning house of Israel who will look on Him whom they pierced, recognise their Messiah (12:10), be delivered from their overwhelming enemies at His glorious appearing (14:2-4), and rejoice in His undisputed reign over them and over the whole world (14:9). Then will commence a thousand years of righteousness, peace and prosperity such as this world has never known, nor can know, until He comes whose right it is to reign (Ezek 21:27), King of kings, Lord of lords, and Prince of Peace. We will return to this again at the end of the next chapter, and also in the final chapter.

These events of the future will be to God and to His Christ occasions of deepest joy, but even now He shares the anticipation of them with His ransomed people prospectively. He has told us of them so that we may enter into His purposes, and order our lives in this present sinful world, so full of strife and sorrow and injustice, in the light of that glorious future.

> *O Zion, when thy Saviour came,*
> *In grace and love to thee;*
> *No beauty in thy royal Lord,*
> *Thy faithless eye could see.*
>
> *Yet onward in His path of grace,*
> *The holy Sufferer went,*
> *To feel at last that love on thee,*
> *Had all in vain been spent.*
>
> *Yet not in vain - o'er Israel's land*
> *The glory yet will shine;*
> *And He, thy once-rejected King,*
> *For ever shall be thine.*

CHAPTER 11

The Day of Atonement

"On that day shall the priest make an atonement for you, to cleanse you, that ye may be clean from all your sins before the Lord" (Lev 16:30).

"So Christ also having been once offered to bear the sins of many, shall appear a second time, apart from sin, to them that wait for Him unto salvation" (Heb 9:28, RV).

> *There in righteousness transcendent,*
> *Lo! He doth in Heaven appear;*
> *Shows the blood of His atonement,*
> *As thy title to be there.*

The Day of Atonement was perhaps the most important day in Israel's calendar, the day of their annual cleansing from sin, still celebrated by religious Jews as *Yom Kippur.* Certain things were done on that day that were done on no other day of the year, as referred to in the New Testament in Hebrews 9:7; notably the entrance of the High Priest within the veil carrying the shed blood to be sprinkled on the mercy-seat. A full account of all the services to take place on this eventful day is given in Leviticus 16, as Jehovah gave it through Moses to Aaron who would perform these services. It is worth reading that chapter before proceeding further. Here, in Leviticus 23, it is viewed especially from the divine side, as the other feasts are, a feast of Jehovah, expressive of the joy derived by Him from the atoning death of Christ.

It is worthy of notice that the Day of Atonement, the day on which the blood was carried within the veil and sprinkled there before and on the mercy-seat, was the tenth day of the seventh month, the month Tizri. At the time of Israel's deliverance from Egypt, the month Abib (or Nisan) which had been the seventh month in the civil year, was changed to the first month (Exod 12:2), and became the basis of the sacred or religious year. On the tenth day of this first month the paschal lamb was to be chosen from the flock, and set apart for sacrifice. Its death on the fourteenth day was the foundation of everything that followed. We have noted before that the Feast of Unleavened Bread, the First-fruits, and the Feast of Weeks, are all dated from the Passover. Now the seventh month begins the second half of Israel's year, and the second series of Jehovah's set feasts also begins.

And here again on the tenth day of this month the blood of a sacrificed victim is the prominent feature, but it will not be used in the same way as in the Passover. There, the blood of the lamb was sprinkled on the lintel and side-posts of the door, to avert the stroke of judgment on Israel's first-born sons. Here the blood is carried within the veil and put on the mercy-seat. In the former case it represents the sacrifice of Christ, appropriated by faith, as that which alone can deliver the sinner from righteous wrath and judgment; but in this feast in the seventh month, it is the blood of atonement presented Godward as that by which His throne is established in righteousness. When God's righteous claims are fully met, the believer is permitted to draw near in spirit to commune with God now, and it is also the ground on which he will enter the presence of God in person by and by.

The sacrifices of the Day of Atonement were (1) a sin-offering and a burnt-offering for Aaron and his house; (2) two goats for a sin-offering and a ram for a burnt-offering for all the congregation of Israel.

The blood of the sin-offering for Aaron and his house was sprinkled on the mercy-seat once, and before it seven times, and above the sprinkled blood a cloud of sweet incense covered the mercy seat. The word "atonement" (which occurs no less than forty-eight times in the book of Leviticus alone) actually means "a covering". The *blood* covered the mercy-seat, and so also did the *cloud* of incense, and in this we have a very expressive type of the *work* and *worth* of the Lord Jesus Christ, in whose blood the believer is made nigh to God, and in whose person he stands accepted. The atoning blood covers all his sin for ever, and the perfectness of Christ encircles his person. The "house" of Aaron stood in the same acceptance as Aaron himself, and thus "the household of faith", the priestly house of New Testament times, composed of all true believers (1 Pet 2:5), stands accepted in Christ and has access even now into the holiest of all (Heb 10:19), and each member is made meet to be partaker of the inheritance of the saints in light (Col 1:12).

In the New Testament, the word *atonement* occurs only once in the AV, namely in Romans 5:11, but there it is actually a mistranslation. The RV renders it more accurately, "We have now received the reconciliation". Atonement was something given to God to make reconciliation possible for men, and that "something" was shed blood; for "it is the blood that maketh an atonement for the soul" (Lev 17:11). Aaron made an atonement for himself and for his household first, and then for the congregation of Israel. It was, we are told, by sprinkled blood on and before the mercy-seat (Lev 16:15). The antitype for us is Christ, "whom God has set forth to be a propitiation, i.e. a mercy-seat, through faith in His blood" (Rom 3:25) - the very same word is used in Hebrews 9:5 for the ark-lid in the tabernacle as is used in this text referring to Christ. And He Himself is the propitiation (the sacrifice offered), as 1 John 2:2 and 4:10 informs us, as well as the propitiatory (the meeting-place), between God and man. All human attempts to explain away the sacrificial and vicarious aspects of our Lord's death, by making it out to be only a supreme act of self-sacrifice in order to win man back to God fail totally. For this leaves sin out of reckoning altogether, and represents man as needing only moral persuasion - not expiation - to make him right with God.

Returning to the ceremonies of the Day of Atonement, we note now that the blood of the goat for the congregation upon which the Lord's lot fell, was likewise sprinkled within the veil (Lev 16:15). Then the sins of the people were confessed by Aaron over a living goat, the scapegoat, and put upon its head, and it was sent away into the wilderness. Thus the claims of Jehovah were all met, the priesthood was established before Him, and the congregation cleansed from all their sins and set at rest. The answer to all this, in so far as it applies to believers today, is fully given in the epistles of the New Testament, where the present cleansing (Heb 10:17-18), acceptance (Eph 1:6), and access (Heb 10:19; 4:16) of believers is made fully known. These are matters to enjoy greatly and to rejoice in here and now.

But the aspect of the truth set forth in this feast has special reference to the future. The Day of Atonement, in its order, comes after the Feast of Trumpets, and before the Feast of Tabernacles. We have already seen that the answer to the Feast of Trumpets, in its application to God's heavenly people, will be the coming of the Lord Jesus as Son of God from heaven to rapture the church; and to God's earthly people it is His coming as Son of Man to earth to reign. The Feast of Tabernacles, as we shall see presently, looks forward to that millennial reign of Christ. The Day of Atonement comes in between. To what event in the future then does it point? Where are we to find its antitype?

Clearly, it must be something after the advent of the Lord, and before His kingly reign. Its answer in respect of the heavenly people is their reception to the immediate presence of God as priests, their establishment around His throne to sing redemption's song (Rev 4-5), and as the servants of Jesus Christ to be manifested before His judgment-seat, to have their service reviewed and their work rewarded (2 Cor 5:10; Rev 22:12). In that full blaze of heavenly light to which the redeemed shall be introduced in the highest heaven, the immediate dwelling-place of God, the value of the blood of Christ will be known by them as it never was before. So also will the marvellous grace of God and the fullness of Christ's redemption be magnified over the exceeding sinfulness of sin. There, amid holy and heavenly hosts surrounding God's throne, the slain Lamb in the midst will still be the object of their worship, and the theme of their song. The eye of God will rest with ineffable delight on that glorified throng, each member of which stands on the merit of the blood of the Lamb, and encircled with His excellence. This will be a rich feast of Jehovah, and the saints themselves will share it, each and all.

> *God's eye of flame that searches all,*
> *And finds e'en heaven unclean,*
> *Rests on each soul in full delight,*
> *For not a spot is seen:*
> *Cleansed every whit in Jesus' blood,*
> *Whate'er its guilt has been.*

The manifestation of the risen saints before the judgment-seat of Christ will be a further answer to this type. At this tribunal, not their salvation, nor the acceptance of their persons, but the character of their service will be under review. The hidden motives and the manifestation of the secrets of all hearts will there be shown in the light of heaven, and revealed to the saints themselves. Then shall they know, even as they are known. The failures of the path, the imperfections of what once seemed so pure and perfect, will be seen as they had never been seen before, and the Master's estimate of it all will be made known. What a change from present estimates of service that day will bring! That which often is so large in men's opinions and obtains their praise, will appear small then! How great will be the recognition and reward for those little acts and hidden deeds known only now to Christ and to God!

> *Deeds of merit as we thought them,*
> *He will show us were but sin;*
> *Little acts we had forgotten,*
> *He will own were done for Him.*

While there will be much to humble the saints at Christ's judgment-seat, there will be nothing to condemn them, for the blood of atonement, the memorial of the ever precious death of the Lamb of God, will forever retain its value to cover all the sins and failures of the Lord's redeemed. Then, after all has been manifested -the good rewarded, the bad burnt up - the saints and servants of God will pass into their places in the kingdom of their Lord, in the perfect enjoyment of rest. And thus the three features of the Day of Atonement will be fulfilled in the risen saints - acceptance, humiliation, and rest.

How all this will enhance the value of the blood of the Lamb! If the devil, the accuser of the brethren, will not at this time have been cast from the heavens, as he will be later (Rev 12:10-11), he may seek to accuse the saints before God on account of the failures of their service as made known at Christ's judgment-seat. If so, he will be answered in this, his last attempt to dispute the saints' title to heaven, by the atoning death of Christ. As it is written, "they overcame him by the blood of the Lamb".

Finally in this chapter we look at the fulfilment of the type in regard to God's earthly people as it is fully and touchingly described in the prophetic Scriptures. Delivered by the sudden appearance of the Lord on Mount Olivet (Zech 14:4), from the allied forces of Antichrist and his confederate kings who at that moment will surround the earthly Jerusalem, they will look up to find that He who is their great Deliverer is Jesus of Nazareth, whom they crucified. His wounded hands and feet will bring back to their mind and conscience that hour when, in their hatred of Him, they cried out, "Crucify Him," and made the awful request, "His blood be upon us, and upon our children." Now they look on Him whom they pierced and mourn. And what a mourning that will be, when "the Spirit of grace, and of supplication" is poured out upon them, and their melted hearts are turned to the Lord (12:10).

Their bitterness and grief passes all description, as they look upon Him whom they had crucified and slain. The deep searchings of heart of Joseph's brethren, as they remembered their cruelty to him, are but a faint illustration of the anguish of awakened Israel in this latter day, when every household and individual apart, alone before God, will mourn their rejection of the Messiah, as one mourns for an only son. When the anguish of Joseph's brethren was at its deepest, the veil that hid him as their brother was removed, and in grace he revealed himself to them as their kinsman and deliverer. In the same way will the glorified Christ reveal Himself and His atoning work to the melted hearts of awakened Israel, and they will turn to find the repose of their souls in the atoning death of the Lamb slain, with the veil taken away from their hearts (2 Cor 3:16). Then it will be that the language of Isaiah 53 will burst from their lips, "Surely He hath borne our griefs, and carried our sorrows; yet we did esteem Him stricken, smitten of God, and afflicted. But He was wounded for our transgressions, He was bruised for our iniquities..." And in that bruising, their healing will be found, for "in that day there shall be a fountain opened to the house of David and to the inhabitants of Jerusalem for sin and for separation and uncleanness" (Zech 13:1, margin). Not a new sacrifice will be required, but the abiding efficacy of the one great sacrifice of Calvary will be extended to them. Thus humbled, cleansed from sin, and brought to God, they will pass into the millennial kingdom, under the benign rule of the Prince of Peace with His heavenly bride.

> *Then thou, beneath the peaceful reign*
> *Of Jesus and His bride,*
> *Shalt sound His grace and glory forth,*
> *To all the earth beside.*

The nations to thy glorious light,
O Zion, yet shall throng;
And all the listening islands wait
To catch the joyful song.

The name of Jesus yet shall ring
Through earth and heaven above,
And all His ransomed people know
The Sabbath of His love.

CHAPTER 12

The Feast of Tabernacles

"The feast of ingathering, which is in the end of the year, when thou hast gathered in thy labours out of the field" (Exod 23:16).

"Hereafter ye shall see heaven opened, and the angels of God ascending and descending upon the Son of Man" (John 1:51).

> *Then the heavens, the earth, and the sea shall rejoice,*
> *The field and the forest shall lift the glad voice,*
> *The sands of the desert shall flourish in green,*
> *And Lebanon's glory be shed o'er the scene.*

The Feast of Tabernacles was the last in the sequence of Jehovah's feasts. It was a season of great joy and rejoicing, a kind of harvest-home, after the harvest and the vintage had been gathered in. Its eighth day, is said to be the "closing festival" (Lev 23:36, RV margin), the last great scene of Jehovah's joy in the accomplishment of His purposes of grace, in which His gathered people are permitted to share.

The antitype of the Feast of Tabernacles, like those of the two that preceded it, is still in the future. Nothing that has yet taken place answers to this season of festive joy; its answer is to be found in the future day of glory, when Christ and His risen saints shall fill the heavens above, reigning over a restored and rejoicing world; when Israel, restored to their long-lost land, and owning Jesus of Nazareth as their Lord and King, shall be the first of the nations; and when, under the peaceful beams of the Sun of Righteousness, risen with healing in His wings (Mal 4:2), the groaning creation shall rejoice and be glad.

The feast was kept for eight days, after the corn and the wine had been gathered in. "Thou shalt observe the Feast of Tabernacles seven days, after thou hast gathered in thy corn and wine" (Deut. 16:13). This detail enables us to see exactly where its antitype comes in, in the dispensational dealings of God in this world.

Israel's harvest consisted of two parts - the corn and the wine. The "corn of wheat" (John 12:24) which fell into the ground and died, but rose again with others associated with it, having the same nature and proceeding from its stem, represents Christ risen from the dead, with all His heavenly people. The ingathering of this harvest has its answer in the whole of the heavenly people, all who share in the first resurrection, being gathered safely home to the garners of heaven. The vintage of the earth (Rev 14:18-19), and the treading of the winepress of God's wrath, has reference to the gathering of Christ's enemies for judgment. After these events have taken place, then the millennial reign of Christ will begin.

In common with the two preceding feasts, the Feast of Tabernacles has an application to both the heavenly and the earthly people of God, although here the dividing line between the celestial and the terrestrial, between things in heaven and things on earth, is not so sharp as in the answers to the previous types. This is because in that coming day of Immanuel's reign, the heavens and the earth will not be as they now are, separated and ruled by opposing forces. For in the day of "the restitution of all things", heaven and earth, and all is in them, will own Jesus Christ as Lord of all.

This day of the restitution of all things is spoken of in Acts 3:21. It must be noted that it has no reference to man's future destiny, although such a meaning has erroneously been read into the passage. The context in Acts 3 limits this restitution to "things which God hath spoken by the mouth of His holy prophets since the world began". This, as every reader of Old Testament prophecy knows, refers to the many passages which speak of times of blessing to the earth and God's earthly people, which will be brought about by judgment on their enemies, not by extended mercy to those who have despised grace. Of these all the prophets speak in glowing words, but they have not a word to say of "a wider hope" for the ungodly, or a ray of comfort to give to those who now despise the gospel of Christ and the salvation it proclaims, by holding forth some after-death probation or evangelization or universal restoration of all men and demons to God, in virtue of the cross of Christ. There will be universal acknowledgment of Christ's Lordship, as Philippians 2:10 informs us, "every knee should bow, of things in heaven, and things in earth, and things under the earth"; but when reconciliation by the blood of His cross is in view, as in Colossians 1:20, it is noteworthy that "things under the earth" are not included in that reconciliation.

In the day of restitution of all things, foreshadowed in the Feast of Tabernacles, the raised and heavenly saints will share the joy and honour of their Lord, when with Him in manifested glory they shall appear as the Bride, the Lamb's wife, to reign for ever.

He and I in that bright glory
One deep joy shall share;
Mine to be for ever with Him,
His that I am there.

To the earthly people, the Feast of Tabernacles points to the joy and rejoicing that awaits them in the latter days on the earth. This feast will then be kept, and all nations will go up to the city of the Great King to celebrate it, as Zechariah clearly states in his prophecy (14:16,17).

"Booths made of palm trees and willows of the brook" reminded the Israelites of wilderness days: the palm - of victories won by His grace; the willow - of the tears wiped away by His hand. Surely, even amidst the glories of heaven, the saints too will remember these, and the memory of them will send forth grateful praise to God and the Lamb. The saints will gladly give the homage of their hearts, as they own the rule of Him who sits upon the throne. To the earthly people, the palm speaks of their share in the triumph and glory of Christ as He reigns from Jerusalem. But in the midst of that scene of triumphant joy, Judah can hardly fail to remember that in days gone by, the Victor's royal brow was once cruelly wreathed with thorns by her hand; and that there, where now the beams of glory shine, stood once the shameful cross of Golgotha, on which her crucified Messiah hung. The memorial sacrifices which they then shall offer on Jehovah's altar, will, like the "willows of the brook", be the memorials of the sorrows and the sacrifice of the Lamb of God. We ourselves sometimes sing of that coming day -

> "Ye saints whose love can ne'er forget
> The wormwood and the gall;
> Go spread your trophies at His feet,
> And crown Him Lord of all."

There is another beautiful representation of the millennial kingdom in its various parts given to us in the transfiguration of the Lord Jesus on "the holy mount", as recorded in the

Gospels. Indeed the Lord told His disciples before He led them up to be "apart" that they would "see the kingdom of God" (Luke 9:27), and Peter speaks of the transfiguration as "the *power* and *coming* of our Lord Jesus Christ" (2 Peter 1:16). In "the excellent glory", high above everything, was God on His throne, and His voice was heard on the holy mount. Above the earth, in heavenly glory, was the person of the transfigured Christ, and with Him, near to Him in that glory, were Moses and Elijah in holy conversation. They respectively represent the sleeping saints who will be raised, and the living saints who will be changed without tasting death, to be with the Lord for ever. This forms the heavenly department of the kingdom. Then lower down, on the earth, yet raised above their fellows, stood Peter, James, and John. They were still in mortal bodies, not in resurrection as the heavenly saints, yet within sight and hearing of the heavenly scene above. This shows us what will be the place of renewed and restored Israel, the earthly people, in millennial days. The earthly Jerusalem "lifted up" and safely inhabited (Zech 14:10), shall bask in the light and glory of the heavenly city (Isa 60:1; Rev. 21:23, 24). We can hardly wonder that Peter, in the midst of such a wonderful scene, said, "It is good for us to be here" - and wanted to erect three tabernacles (booths) on the hallowed spot. But the time for the celebration of the antitype of the Feast of Tabernacles had not come then. They were left with "Jesus only", as we are still until He comes again.

The eighth day, "the last great day of the feast", points on to a period beyond millennial times, for these times, blessed and glorious as they will be, are not the perfect state. Unregenerate man will still be God's enemy, and there will be a last great outburst of Satanic power immediately after Satan is loosed from the prison which has restrained him for a thousand years. He will lead a revolt in which all unregenerate men will share, and this will end in his final judgment (Rev 20:7-9). Then follows the passing away of the heavens and earth, the end of man's long history, as we read in Hebrews 1:10-12 and 2 Peter 3:12-13. Then is the dawn of the eternal day, "the last great day of the feast" - the long Sabbath of Eternity, where, in a new heaven and a new earth, with all things made new (Rev 21:5), righteousness shall have its dwelling-place, and God shall be "all in all".

Beneath Thy touch, beneath Thy smile,
New heavens and earth appear;
No sin their beauty to defile
Or dim them with a tear.

Thrice-happy hour, and those thrice-blest
Who gather round Thy throne;
They share the honours of Thy rest,
Who have Thy conflict known.